MW01244748

Seven Things

You Should Have Learned

But Probably Didn't.

Wanna Try Agin?

Kenneth Shelby Armstrong, M.A., Th.D., Ed.D.

Copyright © 2018

ALL RIGHTS RESERVED.
NO PART OF THIS BOOK MAY BE REPRODUCED OR
TRANSMITTED IN ANY FORM OR BY ANY MEANS,
ELECTRONIC OR MECHANICAL, INCLUDING
PHOTOCOPYING, RECORDING OR BY ANY INFORMATION
STORAGE AND RETRIEVAL SYSTEM, WITHOUT WRITTEN
PERMISSION FROM THE AUTHOR.

Seven Things
You Should Have Learned
But Probably Didn't.

Wanna Try Agin?

Kenneth Shelby Armstrong, M.A., Th.D., Ed.D.

Contents

Foreword   5

Introduction To Your Future. 13

Prepare for Big Things. 21

Select A Profitable Investment. . . . 33

Adopt a Practical Philosophy 41
.

Don't Make Economics Your Main
Focus—Study People Instead. . . . .55 . .

Kick Your Personality into Gear. . . 73
.

Select Peer Partners Carefully. 81

Here's The Trick Never Give Up
That's The Trick Never Give Up. . .89

Other Books By The Author. 104

Foreword

If there is still life in your bones, *this book is for you!* When I read it I felt like Dr. Armstrong wrote it just for me. I think you will get that same feeling, and you will be right. He did write this book for you. He knew what you were looking for.

Do you want to be successful? Read the book and you will be well on your way to a life that you have been striving for.

Do you want to be rich? The book will give you some valuable principles and practices to help you on your journey.

Do you want to read great stories about real people? Read about real people—here, now. These stories are inspiring and in some cases—life changing.

Are you in the market for practical advice on how to enjoy life? If anything, this is a practical book. You will change many things in your life because now you know the magnificent options that are in front of you and available to you..

Do you ever wonder how people can turn their scars into stars? You are suffering with some of life's challenges, you will get hints of how to get out of the hole that you are in.

You may be interested in the author's writing style, or depth of experience in life, or his sense of humor. We'll get to that in a minute. But do this now—this very minute—turn quickly to Chapter One. Don't worry about a book mark. Once you begin, you won't be able to put this book down.

This is one of those *Wit and Wisdom* books you have heard about. Is Stephen Covey's *7 Habits of Highly Successful People* on your desk?

Can you name any of the seven habits without looking them up? Make space next to Covey's book for this one. It doesn't have 381 pages with charts and graphs like *7 Habits* has. But you will soon discover that in its 116 pages are memorable nuggets of truth. And wisdom. And humor.

Covey would have smiled at that one. *Seven* is one of those magical numbers that readers love. More than three. Less than twelve. Perfect.

I personally enjoyed reading Dr. Armstrong's story about a sermon he heard his dad preach in a college chapel service. You will never forget the quote from his father's opening remarks: **"Big Potatoes Come to the Top on Rough Roads."**

Growing up, I was a city boy. I thought potatoes grew on *trees.* It took many years to figure out why potatoes were always covered with dirt. I told you I was a city boy. And pretty dumb.

"The story about **Big Potatoes"** is worth the price of the book! You will tell it to your friends and watch them laugh, especially if they were raised on a farm.

If they ever ask me to write Dr. Armstrong's biography, I am prepared. I have been gathering material about him for several decades. I know of no one who has enjoyed a more adventurous life than my friend. Do you like *adventure?* If you do, buckle your belt and hang on, for the ride of your life.

In 1945 he was drafted into the US Army. Although he was scheduled to fight in the **Battle of the Bulge** in Europe, when the war in Europe ended abruptly he was re-routed to **Japan.** He was one of the first US soldiers to experience the devastation of the **atomic bombs in both Nagasaki and Hiroshima.**

In the mid 1950s, desegregation was the hot issue. So, he decided to try to enroll in an all-black university. He chose **Atlanta University**, a prestigious black institution. He was successful, and became the first white student to explore the reverse reality of racial prejudice.

During the **1960s the Congo massacres** were the headlines of the world's newspapers. He went to the Congo to see the problem for himself and while there he ran into a **guerilla action** and barely escaped with his life.

He visited a **leper colony in Swaziland** and toured the small leper village as a guest of the director of the colony. He recalls being served **luncheon by lepers.**

He was in **Saigon** in the early days of its war, and narrowly missed the bombing of the Army Officers' hotel.

He was in **Havana, Cuba** the week before **Fidel Castro** seized power. A car loaded with rebels sprayed the street with machine gun fire as he ducked into a doorway for safety. He left Cuba quickly.

He visited the site where seven American missionaries were killed on the shores of the **Amazon** river in Ecuador. A side trip lead to hunting **alligators** at midnight. He and a couple of missionaries caught three alligators, and ignored the thousands of **piranha**.

The week after the **Six-Day-War**, he visited Israel and saw several tanks still smoldering on the battlefield. He avoided a rocket attack at the **Sea of Galilee** late one night.

He traveled the upper regions of **Mozambique** where lions and mambas were a constant threat. Natives lived in constant fear of their lives in that harsh environment. He did too.

In the interest of **full disclosure** let me confess that I was privileged to edit the final manuscript of this book. And, my memory is loaded with awesome principles that I will never forget. That same experience is in front of you.

But before you begin, spend five minutes reading this *Foreword.* Did the title of the book grab you? Good. The author has developed great skills in creating titles that draw you into what follows. ***Seven Things You Should Have Learned but Probably Didn't.***

Back to *Seven Things.* I love the "Never Give Up" principle. Every aspiring leader needs to take that essay seriously. Same with the "You Can Succeed" theme. Positive. Forward looking. You will find something practical on every page.

Okay. Are you ready to discover how reading one book can change your mind about the important things of life? Perfect! My five minutes are up. Turn the page.

Thomas Elliott Barnard, M.A., Ed.D.
My Latest book: *Don't Die Above the Ears.*

Introduction To Your Future

As I contemplate wisdom I remember my Dad, who possessed a treasury of wisdom hidden somewhere in his head. His wisdom was not esoteric, it was *common sense wisdom* which is a rare commodity wherever you live. Let me explain.

When I was a junior in a small college in Oklahoma, my father was invited to speak to the student body. I remember the day as if it were yesterday. Nearly a thousand students were present. I was nervous, but most students were simply bored.

My father was introduced by the president of the college. There was no applause and no air of rapt expectation. It was just another day and another speaker to most, but I held my breath in hope that he would not embarrass me by giving some dry discourse.

He was not a towering figure. He did not look like a bishop. He didn't wear an academic robe. I think that most people thought that he was just a farmer. He approached the rostrum slowly and then said softly:

"I have come to tell you that big potatoes come to the top on rough roads."

He paused for what seemed like five minutes and then said again—loudly.

"BIG POTATOES DO COME TO THE TOP

ON ROUGH ROADS."

I looked around me at the students to see how they were reacting, and strangely enough, most of them were staring directly at him. It was as quiet as I had ever known such an assembly to be. Then he began to speak.

"Two farmers lived near to each other out in western Oklahoma. Each had decided to put in a potato crop, and it was harvest time. One farmer had harvested his potatoes and had loaded them into a wagon, and the horses took him to the buyer in the little town only a few miles away. He was back and had a handsome check in his pocket.

"He decided to stop by his neighbor's farm and see how his friend was harvesting his crop. As he drove into the yard, he saw the man sitting on a bushel basket sorting potatoes.

"The sorting of potatoes was important to the price that you got for your crop, for the buyer paid most for big potatoes and the least for small potatoes. And, if you brought them to him unsorted, you got only the small-potato price.

"'How's it going?' the returning farmer asked.

"'It's driving me crazy,' his friend replied. 'Sorting all of these potatoes is a terrible job. You have to make so many decisions. Sometimes I don't know if a potato should go in the *small* basket or the *medium* basket. I'm not sure when a medium-sized potato becomes a big potato. These decisions are killing me.'"

"Well, the other farmer said, 'Hiram, that's not how to sort potatoes. Here's the way to do it. Put all of your potatoes in the wagon, then take the roughest road you can find into town, and by the time that you get there, all the big potatoes will be on top and the small potatoes will be on the bottom, and the middle-sized potatoes will be in the middle, because big potatoes come to the top on rough roads.

"When you get to the buyer, skim off the potatoes on top and sell them to the buyer. Then skim off all the middle-sized potatoes. Then what's left will be small potatoes. This way, you will get top dollar and you won't have to make all of those frustrating decisions.

"Now young people, life is like potatoes. Rough roads are there to sort you out. If you are a small potato you will eventually find yourself at the bottom of life's heap. If you are a big potato, you will surely rise to the top.

"But, if the roads get rough, no small potato can be kept on top, and no big potato can be kept on the bottom.

"Now, everyone of you will be shaken to pieces by rough roads that you can't see now, but they are there in your future. You can't avoid them."

My father went on to explain what it took to be a big potato. He said that a big potato was one who thought and talked about big things.

A big potato was one who dreamed big dreams. A big potato was one who attempted to do big things. A big potato was one who chose friends who were big in mind, big in vision, and big in spirit." His last words were:

"Always remember, big potatoes come to the top on rough roads. Don't moan about your rough roads. Don't mope that you are having a rough journey. Remember, those rough roads are pushing you to the top, and someday you will appreciate even the rough roads."

Wisdom is not always cloaked in silk and finery. Sometimes it wears over-alls. Wisdom does not always speak in Elizabethan English. Sometimes it uses double negatives, and colloquial gibberish. Wisdom is not always phrased in philosophical concepts.

Sometimes it is earthy and common. But it is still wisdom. So respect it wherever you find it. It is still more valuable then rubies. That evaluation comes straight from the Bible, and I have never questioned it.

The smallest of events can be life-changing. It doesn't take much to change the direction of a life. Impact events can be small, but have great consequences. Let me give you a small thought that comes from my wisdom stash.

When I was in the first grade I had to walk about a mile on a railroad track in order to get to school. Every once-in-a-while I could hear the loud roar of a train coming on that track. I would hurriedly get off the tracks and watch the train go by.

Sometimes there would be two or even three big engines pulling the train. And I would alway count how many cars were on that train. The size and power of the train was awesome to experience.

Just before I left the train tracks to get to my school there was a small junction with a diverter handle on it. If the handle was turned one way, the train would veer off and change its direction, and all the cars that it was pulling would follow it.

If it was left alone the great train and all the cars would continue on, ignoring the possibility of going in a different direction.

Life is like that. We head down our tracks in life going at great speed towards a desired destination. But then one small man or some small event, comes out and suddenly turns the handle and you are pushed in a different direction, toward a destination that you had not anticipated.

Then everything changes. Now if they had wanted to change the direction that the train was going, they could have parked a big truck on the tracks. But there are no trucks big enough to stop a couple of locomotives with 100 cars behind them. But with a little engineering, the path of nearly anything can be controlled. And a lot of people will want to control your life too.

My advice is to keep your eyes on the tracks in front of you and watch out for those small diverters. Be your own conductor and keep control of your own train.

Prepare for Big Things

I was fortunate. I learned this admonition early, and this one thing has made all the difference in the world to me.

I was in college when it came to me. The extent of preparation will determine the extent of success. It's like a tree. The extent and depth of the root structure of a tree will determine how high it can grow and whether it will stand when the winds come.

Shallow or surface preparation will result in mediocrity and vulnerability. Extensive and deep preparation is the best guarantee for success and survival.

I heard if from the pulpit, I guess, perhaps from my father, that Jesus lived, studied and prepared for thirty years and only had a ministry of three years. In my youth I puzzled why he didn't start his public ministry at twenty if he was to die at thirty-three.

If he had done that, he could have had an active ministry of thirteen years instead of only three years.

The answer, of course, was that undoubtedly ten years of preparation for three years of ministry was more powerful than thirteen years of ministry with little preparation.

I reasoned that if that principle was good enough for Jesus, it should certainly be good enough for me. So I determined to stay in school or some practical training at least until I reached thirty. And I did it— his way. As I look back I can see that it absolutely does work. It is not always easy, but it is effective.

I earned my A.B. degree in philosophy and as I look back I can see how it helped me deal with issues and ideas. In graduate school I certainly had a lot of new ideas to bombard me.

Two years in the Army, one of which was spent in Japan, was an education in personal and corporate discipline. I developed an appreciation for beauty, grace and antiquity in Japan.

A M.A. degree in philosophy at the university demanded the development of skills of research and writing. What a pain that was!

Seminary was three years of spiritual exploration and preparation for service. I learned that the subject matter is not as important as the kind of professor who taught the subject.

Doctoral study taken in two universities in the fields of sociology and human relations helped balance the study of philosophy.

Later, a second doctorate in higher education helped fashion a professional vehicle for a lifetime of service.

But it was not over. Several years of internship under some outstanding men helped bring it all together and start it slowly moving…forward.

Abraham Lincoln said, "I will study and prepare myself, and some day my time will come." It was true, and it will always be true—the extent of preparation will determine the extent of success.

But schooling and preparation are not synonymous terms. It's common knowledge that many people with extensive education are not prepared to get along in the world in even the most modest manner.

On the other hand, there are some outstanding examples of great and successful men who never went to school but succeeded because they had prepared themselves for success.

It must also be admitted that a lot of do-it-yourselvers never amount to anything. There is a problem here. If preparation won't necessarily prepare you—what will?

The answer is a simple one, and the solution to the problem of preparation can be found in a simple, sociological concept...

"Personality is the sum total of all the

experiences of an individual."

Perhaps the key to this statement is the word experiences. Education can be an experience, but non-educational activities can also be experiences.

But however these are attained, experiences are preparation, and experiences develop personality, and it is ultimately the personality that drives the engine toward success or failure.

To prepare for big things, several experiences will help the personality to grow and develop to the potential for great accomplishments.

Let's look at some of these.

1. Experience great ideas from books.

A book can be a tremendous experience. There is probably no great person that could have achieved greatness without books. The experience of a book can never be taken out or subtracted from a personality. It is always there as a contributing part of that person's success.

I couldn't be me without a few significant books. I would be someone else. A significant part of my personality has come from reading great books.

The Bible, particularity the "Sermon on the Mount", contributed to the structure of my personality, and it can't be eliminated. It is there, and it can't be extracted. It produced experiences for me over too long a time to be ignored.

Of course, I have read lots of books that were insignificant experiences. Some didn't help much, but some produced strong, lasting experiences. Perhaps you can read the same books and have no real experience, but for me the following were powerful enough to stay a part of me. Like *Grapes of Wrath* and...

The Dialogues of Plato,

They Found the Secret,

Language in Thought and Action,

The Governing of Men,

Thoughts That Inspire,

Extraordinary Living for Ordinary Men,

Learning More About Learning,

Move Ahead With Possibility Thinking.

The point is... read! And in your reading, powerful experiences will happen, and you will envelop those experiences into your personality.

2. Experience great emotions through a broad exposure to life.

I remember someone describing another man by saying that he had twenty years of experience in selling. Another man corrected the observation by saying that the man had only had one year's experience, but he had repeated it nineteen times.

This is a way of saying that some people live in a rut, and they repeat the same experiences day after day with the same results. They become dull and unfeeling, and soon they are insensitive to anything that is outside their experiential rut.

Travel! Visit the off-beat places and meet the people. Visit hospitals, concerts, retirement homes, museums, ghettos, lavish suburbs, police stations and synagogues. If you do this, you will feel and grow. I really believe in this. In more than two decades I planned experiences that I believed would help me feel and grow. I don't regret any venture that I had, even though some were dangerous.

2. Experience great emotions through a broad exposure to life.

Personality is the sum total of all of the experiences of an individual. You must plan broad, varied and deep emotions if you are to be prepared to do big things.

We can't all hobnob with the great or even the half-great, but we can select some of those stars in our own universe and meet them and talk to them. In every community there are some outstanding people who are accessible to us. There is a right time, place and method for meeting nearly anyone. A few minutes with a great person can be more fruitful than months or years spent with a dullard.

3. Experience Great People

Don't forget the mail. It is amazing that a simple letter written to a great person will often get a reply.

When I was a young sociology graduate student, I developed a list of the one hundred fifty of the most important living sociologists. I wrote a letter to each of the one hundred fifty men and women asking them to define some key sociological terms for me.

I was amazed that more than half replied, and I have today a collection of letters from some very significant people making statements on some very important topics. Use the mails.

Select and design a way to meet outstanding people. Talk to them, and feel those experiences as they make you grow.

4. Experience Great Deeds.

Try something big. Big deeds prepare you for bigger deeds. Don't wait. Try something significant now. When I was a boy my father asked me one day, "Son, do you know what makes a hero?"

But before I could answer, he said, " Success."

Then he said, "Son, do you know what makes a coward?"

"No, Dad, what makes a coward?" Again he answered "Failure."

Yes, it's true—great deeds are preceded by many other smaller deeds. In fact, a single great deed without preceding smaller ones is probably not possible. So, do something today. That is preparation for something bigger tomorrow.

And, great deeds make people great. Since growth is one of our most important goals, prepare for bigger things by doing big things. The limit of man's capacity, thus pursued, has not been found.

On the other hand, don't ignore the small things. I lived in Africa once and had the fun and excitement of traveling over thousands of miles, visiting the remotest of places. I have sat for hours and watched lions selecting their dinner for the evening. I have watched charging elephants run rampant and have even been chased by a few.

Crocodiles are sinister, and there is hardly anything more frightening to me than big bull African water buffaloes. But I discovered an amazing thing. 90% of the natives of Africa die of insects and bacteria, some of which are so small that they can't even be seen with the naked eye.

Fewer than ten percent of the people die from the attack of a lion, elephant or crocodile. There is great fear of the ferocious beast, but it is the small, tiny germ that is the real killer.

There is life-wisdom in that. Usually, the reason for failure or lack of success is no glaring gigantic fault, but rather a collection of small careless habits, attitudes or actions. We are destroyed more often by little things than we are by great things, so it is important wisdom to remember to observe even the small things.

Prepare for big things but don't forget the small things. Most big things are composed of many small things. Usually, you can't accomplish big things without the mastery of a multitude of smalls things.

Select Your Biggest Investment

Investment opportunities are fascinating. There are so many opportunities—in stocks, oil, real estate, antiques or gold. I've had friends invest in pork bellies, cocoa, matches, bottles and guns.

The fact of the matter is, in the minds of most people, investments like these are considered to be rather commonplace and worthy of the thoughtful consideration of any prudent investor. Many people are always searching for some things to invest in.

The shocking thing is, however, most people never really think about investing in themselves, when the truth is, investing in yourself is the safest of all investments, and it pays the highest return.

> Putting something valuable in your brain is safer than putting something valuable in a vault.

> Mastering new skills can be greater protection than purchasing life insurance.

> Exploring new territories of thought can be more rewarding than searching for a gold mine.

> Tuition paid for significant learning can be a better bargain than dividends earned as a result of other peoples efforts.

The first investment that anyone should ever consider is the fundamental and basic investment in *oneself*. Monies used for personal growth and development are not expenditures; they are investments. Invest in yourself first. I don't think that there is a law against giving investment advice in this area... yet. So let's use a few minutes to consider some sterling advice on investing in yourself.

Invest in learning.

Remain a student all of your life. Start out with a good basic education but never, never graduate from learning, Take courses, attend lectures, establish reading programs, ask questions. Learn new things, at home, at work, or at play. Well-directed learning is one of the fastest elevators to the top. Learning is an escalator that can help you rise faster and farther than you could with just common experience.

Learning need not be formal or confined to certain buildings. It need not take place by a schedule. A teacher is not a necessity. No matter who you are or where you live, learning is abundantly available Seize it where you are.

Buy books.

Books are doors that open up and permit your passage into great and exciting worlds of ideas and experiences. Of course, there are doors that lead to the bedroom, doors that lead to heaven, and doors that lead to hell.

Choose your doors wisely, because they are entrances that will take you somewhere. Before you choose a door, make sure that you really want to visit the place it will take you to. Want to take a trip to possibility land? Then buy Bob Schuller's book *You Can Become the Person You Want to Be*.

Want to take a trip to new zest in living? Then read *Human Life Styling*. Want to take a trip to reality? Then read *The Screwing of the Average Man*. Want to take a trip to abundant life? Then read *Extraordinary Living for Ordinary Men*. It's true. You can go nearly anywhere if you pick the right door. Buy books.

Invest in Travel.

See the world, or at least see your world. A trip to Europe or Mexico or Canada can do more for you than owning a second car or buying a boat.

The United States offers some sights of breath-taking beauty and some experiences of history. In the alleys and avenues of American you will find written the story of human triumph and travail—of hope and helplessness—of opportunity and of oppression. While still a young man, I counted up that I visited more than 60 countries of the world. Based on that experience, I have no trepidation to spread the advice to travel—see—grow!

Dress for Distinction.

Yes, clothes are an investment. Indeed, they are one of your most important investments. "Clothes make the man?" You bet, and the woman too. You will earn more if you dress better. It's true. Clothes pay for themselves over and over again.

I knew a man who lost a $125,000 commission because of his shoes. Here's the story.

I was vice president of a college that was considering hiring a fund raiser to raise millions of dollars from local institutions and wealthy individuals. We had nearly decided to hire a particular candidate who was well credentialed, persuasive and experienced, when one of the committee members asked:

"I wonder if we should choose a man who wears $10 shoes and white socks? Can he really communicate and elicit confidence from large donors?"

The committee, on second thought, decided that he probably couldn't. So the man lost $125,000 because he didn't know how to dress. The pity is that he left not knowing why he lost the contract.

People are passed over for promotion every day because their clothes and general demeanor suggest to those who make the decisions that the person is not "aware, alert, or with it." Clothes not only make the man, they can destroy him too.

What to do about it? Buy two books on dress and grooming. Study them well—like you would a blueprint for a house. Use their directions, and invest in appropriate clothes. Don't cut corners. You are not *spending* money—you are investing in something that will return your investment and pay dividends besides.

Learn to talk and write.

Learning to communicate is a major investment in your future. Learning to express ideas and issues clearly and succinctly can be more valuable than having a rich uncle who is a slightly-ninety years old invalid. The rich uncle may let you down, but the ability to set fourth ideas lucidly and persuasively will never let you down.

Don't give the excuse that it's too late because you didn't get it in school. It's not too late to learn the abc's of speaking and writing. Somewhere near you is a tutor who can help you. There is a group that will let you practice on it.

There are courses available or at least there are books that can be bought that will help you develop this most valuable tool. Success may well dodge your grasp unless you get down to it and learn to communicate with tongue or pen.

Much more could be added, but the point of all of this is: *Invest In Yourself.* If you have to rob someone, rob your savings account. Don't rob yourself. If you have to choose between investments, choose yourself. Let the stock broker wait. Don't send all your money to Washington if you can help it; send some to yourself. Invest In yourself first.

Adopt a Practical Philosophy

Too many people think that philosophy is of no *practical* use. It was Lester F. Ward who said, "The most practical thing in the world is a good theory." To illustrate—a blueprint is only a concept or theory about a house. It is a *dream* that suggests the possibility of a particular kind of house.

A philosophy is a concept, theory or blueprint about life or a phase of it. Who would be foolish enough to start building a house without a concept or blueprint? Who would be foolish enough *to start living without having a concept or philosophy about life?*

A sound practical philosophy is a fundamental necessity for success in living or being. The tragic thing is that too many people want to start living before they have developed blueprints to guide their living.

There is nothing more valuable for achieving success than the development of a good practical philosophy. Let me show you how the development of a practical philosophy has guided the success of some very important people.

1. *The **Push or Pull** Philosophy.*

I sat in the oceanside home of a very wealthy man in Ft. Lauderdale, Florida. The view of the ocean from his living room was spectacular. How I wished that someday I could live in a home like that! So I asked him, "How did you make your money?"

His answer was intriguing.

"Well, you see, I have a philosophy that I live by, and it makes the money for me. I got my first money from an invention. That was my start. Then I was in a position of using money to make money.

"I observed that there were two games being played in life—the *pull* game and the *push* game.

"People who play the *pull* game are asking themselves, 'How can I *pull* a good living out of life? How can I *pull* the most profit out of this deal? How can I *pull* the most for me out of this relationship?'

"Now, when others sense you are playing the *pull* game, they play it too. So life is a tug-of-war. Everyone is trying to pull out of life the most and the best for himself. This game is a hard game, and the stronger take it from the weaker, and most people lose.

"It's terrible, but we are taught from our youngest days to play the *pull* game. Grab all the gusto you can. Look out for number one. Be a hard bargainer.

"But there's another game in town. It's called the *push* game. People who play this game ask themselves, How much can I give to my customers and still stay in business? How much profit can I make for my partners? How can I negotiate this contract so that the other fellow is guaranteed of making as much money as possible?

"Now, when others see that you are really playing the *push* game, they begin to push back. **Give and it shall be given to you**. On all of the deals presented to me, I try to accept those that give the most to the other person.

"I like to invest in projects that will create more jobs for a needy community. I always ask, 'How much can you pay your employees and still make the project work?' I reject those deals that won't permit good wages to be paid.

"I find satisfaction in knowing that people will live in better houses, and their children will live better and have more opportunity. Profits will come as a consequence of this philosophy.

"So I play the *push* philosophy, and everybody wants to go into business with me.

"I get nearly all of the sweetheart deals in this city because people know I have always followed my *push* philosophy. Life has pushed back to me my wealth, because I have always tried to *push* the most and the best to life.

"You can't lose if you generally use the *push* philosophy. I have pushed millions toward others, but others have pushed tens of millions to me.

"You can choose to play either game. If you choose the *pull* game, life will play it too and will try to *pull* from you the most.

"If you play the *push* game, life will play it too and life will *push* back more than you gave it. My philosophy has made me rich."

What a philosophy! I have seen it work. I have tried it, and it works. Too bad that most of us have been taught the *pull* philosophy. We are robbed because we operate from a poor philosophy.

2. The **Team** Philosophy.

It was Andrew Carnegie, father of the American steel industry and a multimillionaire, who said that no man is smart enough to project his influence very far into the world without the friendly cooperation of other men.

A man alone is limited in knowledge, power, time, and experience. Man in concert possesses the synergy of cooperation.

Edison said great men are seldom isolated mountain peaks. They are usually summits of ranges. That's another way of saying that men working together in united effort toward singular goals can accomplish together much more than they could if all worked alone.

Perhaps Carnegie's development of this philosophy of **The Master Mind** is the best example of the value of teamwork that we have. Friends working together with a common purpose can create miracles. If you have not read the Napoleon Hill books that develop this concept, you must, for if you ever dream to do much in life, you will be forced to develop a **team** philosophy.

3. The Hitch Your Wagon to A Falling Star Philosophy.

The Chairman of the Board of one of the major corporations in America espouses this philosophy. Some time ago in conversation with a friend he was asked how he had secured his position and how he came to sit on so many other corporate boards.

His reply was to relate his operational philosophy.

"When I was younger I sat on boards of several small companies, and I observed that because of politics, or mistakes, or changes in company philosophy, the directors would decide that a new president was called for, and the old one would be summarily fired. These firings could get pretty bloody sometimes.

"I also observed that, when a president was fired, he suddenly became almost friendless. His loyal staff quickly stepped on the new bandwagon. The new president grabbed the reins of power, and the old one lost his power, prestige and authority. Sometimes he was open prey to employees or board members who may have secretly resented him for a long time.

"Being unprotected, he caught the criticism, blame and abuse of everything that had gone wrong in the past. Old friends were somewhat uneasy about being seen with him after his firing. Now he was alone and stripped of defenses and supporting friends.

"As I observed these happenings, it occurred to me that, at this time more than any other, this man needed a friend. Whether he was right or wrong was immaterial; he was suffering and lonely and needed someone just to talk to.

"I decided to make a concerted effort to be a friend to these men at the time of their greatest need. After a firing I would plan to spend as much time as possible with the man during the following weeks.

"Even on occasions when I voted to fire the man myself, I moved toward him, and sometimes I received his anger and abuse. But I would continue to move toward him and offer a hand of friendship.

"I began to observe later that these men started to come back. They would rise again and show up as president of another company, and sometimes it would be a larger company than the one that they had been fired from.

"The same qualities and strengths that got those men to the top in the first place caused them to rebound even higher the second time around.

"Now, here's the payoff to this philosophy. When the men hit the top again, they remembered that the one man who stood with them when they were falling was myself. And, soon they found a way to get me named a director of the new company, because everyone needs a friend.

And friends who are with you when you are ***down*** are the best kind to have around when you are ***up***.

By hitching my wagon to falling stars I have soared pretty high."

There's no doubt that this simple philosophy has been the basis of this man's success. It's true. There is nothing more practical and workable than a good philosophy.

4. The **Find Someone to Serve** Philosophy

One of the most powerful and practical philosophies that I have ever heard is this one articulated by General Eisenhower. Somewhere along the line he developed the concept that the best launching pad for success was that of becoming an assistant to a great person and serving him well.

Eisenhower reasoned that, if you served close to a great person, you would have access to the experiences and events of that person. You would be able to observe firsthand the qualities that made him great. You could watch him make decisions and react to ordinary events and crises. Their experiences would become your experiences. He concluded that a young person could advance his progress rapidly by getting in this unique posture of learning.

Eisenhower concluded too that, if you served the man well and stayed close to him, when he needed someone for an important job, he would see you and perhaps tap you for the assignment.

It is not well known that, throughout his military life, Eisenhower practiced his philosophy as well as he preached it. He served as assistant to two of America's greatest generals. For a period he was aide to General Douglas McArthur and observed firsthand the power of this military genius. As assistant to McArthur he learned more than any school could ever teach him.

Later he served as aide to General George Marshall, the number-one general of the Army and later author of the Marshall Plan. The diplomacy, compassion and practical logic of General Marshall was well observed by Eisenhower and he incorporated it into his own personality.

One wonders what would ever had happened to General Eisenhower if he had never served under McArthur and Marshall. Without the learning and experience derived from serving *close* to these two great men he probably would never have succeeded as he did. Likewise, without the performance of serving these two men *well*, he would never have been promoted to assignments of greater responsibility.

President Eisenhower's very practical philosophy of finding someone to serve, paid great dividends. And, indeed, it still works. It works in the factory or in the office. It works in schools and in the church. It works in business or in charity. There is nothing more practical than a good philosophy.

5. *Build a System* Philosophy.

Most people work *hard,* but most people do not work *smart.* Most people just work—they trade time for dollars. And, when they run out of time, the dollars quit coming.

On the other hand, some people build systems that, in themselves, produce dollars. A business is a system. If it is put together right, it will continue to produce money long after the creator of the system is dead and gone.

I have a friend who believed in building systems. He was not willing to trade his time for a salary. He knew that his time was limited, and, when his time ran out by reason of illness or age, the money would stop flowing.

He believed that there was little security in working in the other man's system. He knew that this labor and ingenuity would only strengthen, the other man's system, but it would deplete his own time.

He decided to build a business—a system. He worked hard year after year building the system. He paid his employees more than he himself took out of the business. For years he was nearly the lowest paid employee of the company.

But the difference was that he *owned* the system, and eventually he stopped work, and the company kept paying him better and better.

When the employees stopped working, the system stopped paying them, because they didn't own it. They had been content to trade time for dollars, and they ran out of time.

My friend told me that he developed this philosophy when he was a very young man and that he had never worked for any other man in his entire life.

The fruit of his labor was all conserved for his own use. This philosophy made him wealthy.

There are dozens of other practical philosophies that have made people successful. Perhaps the ones recounted here do not fit you, but be assured that there is a philosophy somewhere adaptable to you. And a good practical philosophy is a prerequisite to success. Prepare your own practical philosophy, and begin developing it now.

Don't Make Economics Your Main Focus—Study People

Human behavior is the fabric of success. There is no success apart from the behavior of one or more people.

What people do—behavior—creates heaven or hell. Behavior must be the primary field of study for any person committed to succeeding.

Where did we learn to understand human behavior? In the school? In the home? In the alleys? The answer is probably yes to all of these! We learn about and study human behavior from our earliest days, in every laboratory of our human experience.

But, the tragic thing is: we *never learn enough.* Until the day we die, we are perplexed by the behavior of those near us, and quite often we are puzzled by our own behavior.

It's a subject matter that we never master, and until the day we die we seem never to proceed beyond being an elementary student. No one ever graduates.

Nevertheless, let's banish the pessimism of those words and take another crack at understanding ourselves and others. If we can make progress in this area, we can make progress toward success.

If we don't make progress in this area, we *can't* make progress toward success. Cavett Robert says that 12½ percent of success is due to **product** knowledge, and 87½ percent of success is due to **people** knowledge. If we are to move ahead, we've got to understand people.

There are two basic philosophies of human behavior prevalent in the experience of the common man. Psychologists call the most common one, and the most dominate one, the *behavior* or *stimulus-response* theory. This theory is what most of us have been taught, and this is what most of us practice.

We are taught to believe that *behavior is the result of forces exerted upon it.* Behavior is the *effect,* and something else is the *cause.* Our most natural questions are these: **I wonder what's eating him? What's bugging her? I wonder what made him do that?** The assumption inherent in this theory is that behavior is the result of some external force acting on the behaver.

It's kind of a **pool table** theory. We believe that people are like billiard balls. If you hit them at the right angle, they will bounce off in a predictable direction.

The **Master Motivator** is, therefore, the guy who can use bank shots and caroms to make people do anything he wants them to. The **pool table** theorists study the techniques and skills of saying the right thing or doing the right thing to make people act in a prescribed and preferred manner.

Now the problem with this theory of human behavior is not that it is *wrong,* but rather, that *it is only partially right.* Of course these manipulative techniques often work, and yes, there are **Master Motivators** who control people as pawns, but there are some fundamental errors in relying on this theory to change behavior.

It is true that, quite often, you can exert a pressure on another person, and he or she will behave in a certain way. But when the pressure is removed, will his or her behavior continue on line?

Not every time. Often when the manipulative force is removed, the behavior returns to its original pattern. To keep the behavior on line you have to keep the manipulation present, and in most cases, you have to increase its intensity.

You can manipulate children to eat their food with promises of candy. You can manipulate salesmen to work hard by having a contest with prizes. You can manipulate religious conversions by threatening or scaring the sinner.

You can manipulate people into liking you by smiling or slapping them on the back. You can manipulate bosses to promote you by playing to their vanities or weaknesses.

But the big question is what happens to behavior when you remove the reward or stimulation? Does the child still eat his food willingly? Do the salesmen still work hard? Does the sinner forsake his sins and pursue righteousness when no longer threatened or scared? Do people still like you when you must correct them or discipline them? Does the boss still promote you when you aren't a yes man?

Using behavioral theory and manipulative techniques may work on the short run, but they really won't in the long run, because they have an inherent defect. The behavior is changed, but the *behaver* isn't. Until the *behaver* is changed, the behavior will continue to move back to its natural performance.

In my first two years of college I made D's and F's in all of my subjects. Believe me, I was subject to gigantic forces of manipulation. I was enticed to do better. I was threatened if I didn't. I was offered prizes if I would bring up my grades. I was threatened with expulsion if I didn't. No amount or kind of manipulation worked. My effort and my grades remained unchanged.

My last two years of college I made all A's and B's. What happened? It's simple. I changed. So my behavior changed. When I changed, my ways of looking at school and studying changed, and so my behavior was a natural outgrowth of my new self. I didn't need manipulation to keep my behavior on line. I was on line, so my behavior was on line.

It is important to understand that behavior may be the result of forces exerted on the *behaver*, but to rely on that theory conclusively is to limit your understanding seriously.

Likewise, to use this theory as a pattern for manipulating people to behave in certain ways is a mistake. Once you start manipulating, you have to keep on manipulating.

You should broaden your understanding of human behavior by considering the second, and probably the more practical, of the theories. This theory is called the Perceptual Theory. Its simplest statement is that **behavior is the function of perception**. People act out of **perceptual patterns**.

*1. Man can initiate his own behavior. He doesn't have to be influenced or caused externally to do anything. He can be a **cause** as well as an **effect**.*

2. Man always behaves in a manner that is consistent with his view of what protects or enhances his self-organization.

3. Behavior is a function of man's perception of what's best for himself in any given situation.

This theory of human behavior holds that all behavior is the result of *the way the behaver looks at* a given situation. It is the perception or viewpoint that determines behavior. And the key to understanding a person's behavior is finding out how she is looking at the situation. You must get behind her **eyeballs** to see how she is looking at things if you are to understand her behavior.

Of course, a gigantic question is, **What makes people see things the way they do?** The answer to this problem according to this theory, is that there are at least six isolated **perceptual determinants**. That is to say, there are six factors that determine our perceptions and cause us to see things the way we do.

Belief.

We may see certain things because a particular belief may control what we see. To illustrate: If I believe that a person really dislikes me and is a genuine enemy, he can hardly do anything that I will see as good. If he brings me a box of candy as a gift, I wonder what he's up to. If he gives me a compliment, I wonder what he's trying to get.

Conversely, if I am convinced that someone really likes me, he can walk up, hit me and exclaim, "How are you doing, you old skunk?" and I'll chuckle and enjoy it. On the other hand, if I believe that he doesn't like me, the slightest edge to his voice can be an affront.

If I believe that a person is untrustworthy, in every act he performs I see some devious scheme. He can give a large gift to a church, and I'm convinced that he is maneuvering to get into someone's pocket.

Belief is one perceptual determinant. What I believe about people, myself and the world determines my perception of people, myself and the world, and that perception determines my behavior. The second behavioral determinant is:

Need.

I see what I ***need*** to see. If I have a strong need for acceptance, I see, in the slightest gestures of others, acts of acceptance or rejection. If I have a strong need for love, I become a patsy for any old line of blarney.

If I have a strong need for orderliness or perfection, I see the small flaws or inconsistencies in a great idea before I see the greatness of the idea itself.

Why do some people see every scrap of paper or piece of dirt while walking down a hallway while others wouldn't even notice a mud puddle in the living room?

Albert Einstein said, "Stay away from negative people. They have a problem for every solution."

The particular needs of each individual may determine how he or she sees any event or opportunity. Needs can determine perception, and behavior is the function of perception.

Attitudes.

An attitude is really an emotionalized belief. An attitude is rather like the climate of a personality. It is an emotional climate.

Have you ever had a feeling of impending doom or disaster, and at that precise moment the telephone rang? Your stomach tightened, and with real fear you answered the phone fully expecting to hear something terrible?

Have you ever been completely exuberant about something that had just happened and the phone rang, and you picked it up happily and spoke a cheery hello? Your attitude of the moment quite often determines the way that you look at any immediate event.

When you are **up** the chatter of kids in the home can be seen as homey and indeed comforting. When you are **down** the same thing can be seen as an intolerable annoyance. Attitudes affect your perceptions, and behavior is the function of perception.

Values.

Our personal values also determine the way that we look at things. If a person values absolute precise honesty, the small exaggeration of a story by a colleague is seen as a blatant expression of lying. If a person values frugality above all, he is likely to see salesmen as reckless squanderers of company assets.

If one has strong values of modesty, simplicity and humility, the normal behavior of an extrovert will drive the person up the wall. On the other hand, people who value strong expressions of friendship or free and enthusiastic interplay, may see in the reserved person a coldness, hostility, or snobbishness in all his behavior.

What we hold in values can condition our perceptions, and perceptions accordingly control our behavior.

A group of men went to lunch together one day. They were casual but not close friends. It was a pleasant affair for all. The waitress brought the bill and each looked to see what his portion was. They all produced their share of the bill.

As they were leaving one said **What about the tip?**

Immediately, another man said "I'll take care of it." He walked back a few steps and took out his wallet and pulled out a $50.00 bill and layed it on the table for the waitress. He then turned to follow the rest of the men who were in conversation.

One of these men was thinking to himself, "Wow, he should have left $20.00 at most. I'm sure glad he's not spending my money. At most he should have left $20. That's foolish." The speaker of those words was a C.P.A. He valued frugality and the careful use of money. He would never go into business with that foolish salesman.

Now the salesman had observed that the waitress seemed to be anxious and under some kind of pressure. He surmised that perhaps she was having some kind of trouble at home. He thought that she might be having financial problems because waitresses don't make very much money. So he left a larger tip than usual. Perhaps that $50.00 could help solve some of her problems. He felt good about himself.

Self-experience.

Our past self-experience determines the way we look at present conditions or events. If we have experienced a lot of failures, we see in each new venture the very real possibility of failure. If we have experienced a lot of success, we see opportunity everywhere. If we have suffered at the hand of a lawyer or doctor, we see in every future encounter with them, the potential of danger.

Past experience is one of the most powerful determinants of perception, and, since behavior is the function of perception, we are too often enslaved by our past and not free to see and accept the generous future that is really there.

To illustrate the point, a certain man, Tom, found a very promising financial venture, but after studying the cost that it would require, concluded that he needed a partner to go in on the deal with him.

First, he thought of a dentist friend of his as a possible partner. He went to him and laid out the whole plan. Within seconds the dentist replied,

"No, George, I don't feel good about it. The last couple of deals I've entered, I've lost a lot of money. I think I'll sit this one out."

The real problem with the dentist was that he had lost a lot of money on past ventures, and he saw in this new venture another possibility of losing more money. His past experiences forced him to see this new one as being another bad experience. He just couldn't see the benefit.

Tom understood the dentist's reaction, so he thought of another friend who might be interested in the deal. Sam was a very successful farmer and was always interested in good investments. Tom called him on the phone.

"Sam, this is Tom. Sam, I have just run into a new deal and I need a partner. It's that old parcel of land across from the golf course and I'm certain we can buy it and sell it and make $50,000 each. I even have someone who may be interested in it. We would both have to put up $50,000, but I feel confident that we can get our money back plus the $50,000 profit."

"Count me in Tom, When do you need the money? I can call Jim down at the bank and he will write you a check immediately."

Now a major reason that the offer was so acceptable was that Sam had joined many such ventures as this one and he had always made money. Thus his past successful experiences permitted him to see this venture as a another opportunity for making more money. Behavior is a function of perception.

Threat.

Threat can also determine perception and affect behavior. Have you ever walked down a dark country lane and actually seen beast after beast looking out at you and ready to spring? I have seen more movements and dangerous eyes peering stealthily at me while walking in the dark, and running really didn't help for they could always run just as fast as I could.

Where there is threat, there are always abnormal perceptions of danger and ominous visions of harm. Threat can create warped perceptions of even friendly gestures, and strange behavior results.

The point that perceptual theorists make is that to really understand behavior, you must go to the **determinants of perception**, for these are the things that determine behavior.

What does the person *believe* about himself, others, and the world?

What does the person *need*
to enhance or protect himself?

What is the person's *attitude*
at the particular time?

What *values* control the person?

What has the person *experienced*
most deeply or most recently?

What *threatens* this person?

These determinants are the key to specific perceptions and ultimate behavior.

What are the implications of this theory of human behavior? To understand human behavior you must go to the perceptions of the human behaver. To influence human behavior you must also engage the *determinants of that behavior.*

Of course, this is harder, but it is more permanent. Once you change the way that a person looks at things, you can leave and know pretty well that the behavior will remain constant.

Whether you are a teacher or preacher, salesman or administrator, friend or antagonist, the place to start in understanding or influencing others is the six determinants of perception. Master these, and success is closer to you than you know.

Kick Your Personality Into Gear

The Nuclear Bomb in your arsenal of success may be your brain, but the delivery system is most certainly your *personality*. A country would be foolish if it spent billions of dollars creating a nuclear bomb, if it had no way of delivering it to a target.

The analogy holds true. It is just as foolish to spend all of your time perfecting knowledge and understanding, if you don't have the personality to use the knowledge and understanding in an effective way.

Some serious effort toward the development of personality is a requirement for the one who pursues success. Let's consider some principles that can help you to develop your personality.

Be Yourself.

Take pride in the fact that you are an individual of immense worth and value. Being born in Boston makes one no more valuable than being from Broken Bow, Oklahoma. Take pride in who you are, and don't let who you are be deprecated by anyone. Believe it!

Hold to your own integrity. Don't sell out to be someone else. Don't even wish to be someone else. Recognize the uniqueness that you possess, and don't lose that uniqueness for anything. Hold out your sign. This person is not for trade or sale.

Observe Others.

It's one thing to lose your own identity and become someone else, but it's quite another thing to select fine qualities that you see in others and bring them into the organization of your own self. Don't change the core-you, but do add to yourself many of those fine qualities that you observe in others.

Move Out and Meet New People.

We quite commonly absorb into our personalities those traits and qualities of the people that we spend time with.

An old Persian proverb says "Run with dogs and you will soon learn to howl," The opposite is true also. Spend time with people of grace and intelligent conversation, and you will soon assimilate into your own life some of those qualities.

Move out and meet *action* people, people who do things—who get things done. Move out and meet *contemplative* people, people who think and reflect on the deeper and more subtle issues of life. Move out and meet unique people—people who are crosscurrent to your normal life and who march to the beat of a different drum.

Move out and meet young people, or old people, or black people, or foreign people. In each encounter with another person you will find created a new dimension in your own being.

Learn to Speak and Write.

That seems trite to say, but it is significant. Too many people just try to transmit messages without any real concern for clarity or quality. How you speak or write is tremendously important, and any laborious effort to refine your speaking and writing will be greatly rewarded.

Become alert to how you sound in daily conversation. Tape your speech, and listen to it over and over. Practice diction and phraseology.

One of the great books of my memory is one written by Elwood Murray, *Your Speech Personality.* Dr. Murray stressed the fact that speaking is the major expression of personality, *and* it is capable of development.

Take a class in public speaking or sign up for the **Carnegie Course**. But, whatever you have to do— develop your speaking and writing skills.

Control Your Mind.

The mind is a power factory capable of producing tremendous energy. Uncontrolled, it can destroy. Controlled, it can create.

There are three things that interact in our lives. *Feeling, thinking, doing.* I look at the three like a train engine with two following cars.

> *When **Thinking** is the engine and **Doing** and **Feeling** follow, great strides are made toward success.*

> *When **Feeling** is the engine and **Thinking** and **Doing** follow, you wander on an erratic course, because feelings are fickle.*

> *When **Doing** is the engine and **Feeling** and **Thinking** follow, the progress is slow and tiring. The ideal is to **think** first, **do** second, and **feel** third.*

By fastening your mind on elevating and promising things—you go upward. By observing bad things you descend. The greatest recipe for health of mind was established by St. Paul.

"Whatsoever things are true, whatsoever things are honest, whatsoever things are just, whatsoever things are pure, whatsoever things are lovely, whatsoever things are of good report; if there be any

virtue, and if there by any praise, think on these things."

Develop PMA.

The power of a Positive Mental Attitude has been stressed by so many that it hardly seems necessary to repeat it. On the other hand, since it is an essential and not a mere luxury, an overemphasis hardly seems possible.

The book *Move Ahead With Possibility Thinking* is a must for anyone who really seeks success. The author of that story was a minister who started preaching on the tar roof of a drive-in theater and ultimately created a beautiful church called the Crystal Cathedral. His adventure illustrates the power of positive thinking.

PMA can take you from a peanut farm to an oval office. (President Carter)

PMA can take you from an Ohio farm to the moon. (Neal Armstrong)

PMA can propel you from a haberdashery in Kansas City to the White House. (President Truman)

PMA can take you from a farm and put you anywhere that you want to be. (George Washington)

The Key?

PMA.

Mobilize your personality. You have a dynamo in you that wants to do great things. It needs a good delivery system, and your personality is the vehicle that carries your ideals, beliefs, and commitment. Move ahead. Start now. You can succeed.

Select Peer Partners Carefully

"No man is smart enough to project his influence very far into the world without the friendly cooperation of other men," said Andrew Carnegie. In anything that we do of any significance, we are necessarily bound to a system of partnerships. Therefore, the careful selection of these partners is vital.

We should probably be aware of the fact that things that we would not want in ourselves, we would not want in a partner. That, of course, establishes a pretty high standard, but it is a reality that we cannot ignore. Ira Hayes says that there are five things that destroy success.

Carelessness,

Laziness,

Indifference,

Forgetfulness,

Temptation.

These are qualities that we certainly do not want to see in ourselves or in our partners.

The apostle Paul speaks of the problem of being *unequally bound together* with others. It makes sense that, if the partners of any endeavor hold conflicting motivations or methods, the project is not destined for greatness. Indeed, it may be headed for disaster.

Taking a hint from perceptive psychology, we might conclude that there is the greatest chance for success where partners see things similarly. Moving back to the guidelines of the perceptual determinants, we might ask some key questions.

1. Are our *beliefs* pretty well similar?

2. Do our *needs* conflict?

3. Are our *attitudes* compatible?

4. Do we share common *values?*

5. Is the range of our *past experience* not too dissimilar?

6. Does *threat* control either one to an unhealthy degree?

If the perceptual determinants of both partners are not too similar, then one can expect similar perceptions and thus behavior can harmonize. On the other hand, if beliefs, needs, attitudes, values and past experience are polar, then perceptions will be widely divergent, and behavior will not likely be parallel.

What should one ordinarily look for in a partner? What traits should be common to all partners in a project? Consider these.

1. A natural inclination to work hard.

Look for someone who willingly puts in long hours working to accomplish a task or reach a goal. This hard work, however, must be productive, not just a spinning of the wheels.

2. A realistic appreciation for money.

Look for someone who appreciates money but who is not in awe of it. The desire to acquire is not a sin. A man who does not want money is an exception.

3. The ability to learn rapidly.

Since learning is life-long, skill in learning is a great aid. Look for a man who reads broadly and consistently.

4. A willingness to compete.

I would want to work with a real competitor, one who wants to *WIN*. Noble goals require considerable struggle, and usually they are available only to people who are willing to strive hard.

5. A commitment to self-improvement.

I plan to grow and improve the rest of my life, and I don't want to be yoked to a partner who is not committed to growth. If I grow and she does not, the gap between us will grow and soon a parting will result.

6. Courage.

There is always enough risk and threat in any great project to strike terror into the timid heart. Courage to face danger and perhaps failure will be required on the rough road.

7. An attention to details.

Attention to small things is a fundamental requirement for success. Follow through is great for the golf swing, and it is great for business, too.

8. The ability to organize time.

Look for that person who has goals and has a plan for achieving them. He organizes his work schedule against a clock and a calendar, and he controls the schedule.

9. Persistence.

This is the "never say die" man: he never gives up. He gets his motivation from within. Ira Hayes says one-half of all people fail because they quit doing something because someone didn't like it.

*10. The ability to move **with** people.*

Some people move **against** other people. They are rash and rough. Some people move **away** from people. They are frightened and do not want to get involved. Some people move **with** people. They are interested and involved with those around them.

No one can possess all of these characteristics to the ultimate, but neither should anyone be void of them. A careful consideration of these traits in yourself or your potential partner will save a lot of heartaches and perhaps some heartburn too.

There is a sign in Oklahoma on a remote country road that reads, "Select your ruts carefully--You'll be in them for the next twenty miles." There's a sign on the road to success that reads, "Select your partners wisely—you'll be traveling with them through many rough miles." I wish I had learned this earlier in life.

Never give up

That's the trick

Never give up

If a man *can* be defeated, he probably *will* be defeated. There is something predatory about life. It finds a way to seek out and devour the weak and unwitting.

Success is not a natural response to ordinary living. Success is an extraordinary achievement evolved out of extraordinary struggle. Most people lose in life. Few people succeed.

It doesn't have to be that way, but too often it is that way. Faint hearts and faint commitments are omens of failure. Opportunities grasped loosely more often than not will be seized and lost.

It is also true that neither success nor failure is *final*. Success can be built on top of colossal failure, and failure is omnipresent with our most exalted victories.

Neither is final. If eternal vigilance is the price of freedom, **tenacity** is the price of success. You simply must—never give up.

If you are enjoying the peak of your success, you cannot give up, because when you stop rowing the current grabs you, and it moves you where *it* will.

If you are suffering massive failure, you cannot give up, because others have shown us that some of our greatest empires have been built over the ashes of defeat. You can never give up.

There used to be a popular TV program called KAZ that I tried to never miss. KAZ was a juvenile delinquent and was sent to prison for crimes for which he was admittedly guilty. During those prison days he studied law, and when he came out, he passed the bar and became a practicing lawyer.

The drama on the show always begins with KAZ getting the most impossible cases. In nearly every episode it seems that there is no possible solution to the case.

It was fun to watch KAZ fight and struggle to win against stacked decks and powerful opponents. But of course he did always win. But winning is not the highlight of the show.

The real highlight of each show was that moment when things looked darkest, and there seemed to be no way for him to get out of the mess—KAZ used his motto.

Never give up

that's the trick

never give up

I watched that show each time that I could, just to hear that line.

Never give up

that's the trick

never give up

If you can be defeated, you probably will be defeated. But, if you refuse to be defeated, you cannot possibly be defeated. Somehow, some way, some time, out of complete ruin, defeat, or destruction, an embryo of success can form and soon a robust living, breathing winner will crawl out and make his swath in a new life.

I know it's true because I've seen it happen. And, as I understand it, that was what Jesus was talking about.

> Jesus told men in captivity that they could be free and nothing could keep them enslaved.

> He told failures that they could be reborn and have a new clean successful life.

> He told harlots that they could become clean again.

> He told sinners that they could become holy.

He told weak men that they could become strong.

He told the poor that they could have abundance.

He told the dull and the dead that they could become born again and have new life and have it more abundantly.

The secret is to **Never give up**. Never surrender to the apparent inevitability of conditions. The fact that you are down in the deep, murky waters of failure may only be a clue to how far you will pop out when you do.

Just, **Never give up**. Failure is not comfortable, but it has its contribution to make. Success may give *motivation,* but failure can give *wisdom.* Success can offer *energy,* but failure can provide *strength.* **Never give up!**

Now, I have personally known some success. Indeed, perhaps I had too much, too soon. At one time lead seemingly turned to gold at my touch. I made money easily. I received advancements far faster than my readiness should have permitted.

I was acclaimed and ascribed attributes that I did not possess. I was sought after and spoiled with recognition. I enjoyed around me always—the trappings of a most apparent success. I wanted for little, and I needed nothing.

But I discovered that success can melt quickly. It can fade as a wisp, and the fresh touch of it on your cheek can be lost, and be as though it never happened. Failure can close over success like a shroud, and your once vibrant success can lie like a corpse—an ugly dead corpse.

And I know it can happen to anyone. Indeed it has been my experience that all really successful people have also known the blight of failure, but happily it is not usually permanent. It doesn't have to be.

Let's Talk Failure!

Ask someone who has just come through a time of failure. They will probably not want to talk about it, but they remember it. They will not forget it. They never prepared for it. But it came like a tornado. It is never silent. It is never benevolent.

When failure wipes it all away, what do you do with the empty days—when dreams and success are yanked away—when recognition, respect and reputation are colder than yesterday's ashes—when the phone never rings, and nobody ever writes?

What do you do when newspapers blare your folly? What do you do when your closest friends ignore you and the prophets of doom are crowned kings?

What do you do when the money is gone, and when all that you have worked for is in jeopardy. How do you make a living? What do you do in the meantime?

You suffer.

I have suffered. Oh, how I have suffered! Nobody knows how I have suffered. Once my dreams evaporated. My hope became as thin as paper. I thought that I would never escape failure's horrible clutches. .

But I have learned that almost anyone will have a period in their lives when they suffer. Anyone will suffer, but besides your suffering, you still get hungry and sleepy and you go on living...barely.

Once my phone rang off the hook with invitations to speak or serve in some capacity, but now, it never rang. *Once* my mail was voluminous with commendation and appreciation but now no letters came. I was in the long dark tunnel.

Lonely, I had never been lonely before, but now I had lost nearly every friend that I had ever had. A few reached out to comfort, but I was so wounded and deformed that I couldn't accept that which was offered.

Fear? I had never known fear before, but now I knew *terror*. Dragons roared from the darkness. Ominous newspaper articles circulated, and the threat of the unknown never let me rest.

Self-deprecation? I was vicious in my condemnation of myself. I lost all self-respect. All of the blame for everything I heaped on myself. It was an internal burden that I would always carry. It seemed apparent that it would follow me all of the days of my life. I lost meaning and value in living. Each day was like the last. Miserable.

A Long, Dark Tunnel

I remembered one time years ago in Colorado, hiking with my eight year-old daughter along an old abandoned railroad track built through a mountain.

We approached it cautiously but the promise of adventure shoved us on. We went in and soon came to a curve in the tunnel where in looking both back and forward we could see no light. It was dark looking in, and it was even darker when we entered.

Obviously, there was an end to the tunnel somewhere round the bend, but we couldn't see it. We stumbled into the darkness and fell once or twice but we kept going.

Pretty soon the light was gone from the point where we had entered, and, as yet, there was no sign of any exit. We held to each other and stumbled on.

A bird flew past, but the sound of those small wings echoed like the wings of a giant vulture. Daddy was as uneasy as daughter.

Soon, we saw a dim glow. It was a suggestion—just a suggestion—that there really was an exit out of the tunnel. In a few moments, a light appeared a long way off, but it was there, and we knew that everything was O.K. We ran out of the tunnel and bathed in beautiful sunlight.

On another occasion I walked through a tunnel of a different kind and I walked alone. There was no possibility of going back, and there was only darkness ahead. I tried to have faith and hope. I searched for some sign of promise, but there was only darkness. That was sure one long tunnel.

I approached the end of the tunnel timidly. I had been in darkness so long that my eyes were not accustomed to the light. I couldn't see too well, but there it was—abundant, brilliant light.

Then, I saw it clearly. The light was God and he had been standing there all the time waiting for me to come out and live again. He had heard my footsteps long before I had seen the light.

He was light, and love, and hope, standing there waiting for me.

Now I can run again and not stumble. I can see beauty and not fear. I can live freely and abundantly. For if He makes you free, you will be free indeed.

I have failed, but I can succeed. I have sinned, but I can become holy. I have hurt others, but now I can help others. I have been blind, but now I can see. I have failed, but I can succeed.

Never give up

that's the trick

never give up

But just for a moment, let's forget Failure. Let's talk about **success**. You may not have recognized it, but you have been accumulating ideas and techniques which can be woven into a beautiful pattern of Success.

Already you have accumulated parts of a blueprint. That's right. You *own parts of a blueprint*. No one can take them away from you. You own them.

Yes, you'll encounter rough roads, just as I did. What will you do? Will you pull off to-avoid the bumps and let life and success pass you by? Or, will you remember that:

Big potatoes always come to the top on rough roads.

And, no tunnel lasts forever. So just move ahead. Think you are alone? Don't worry; someone is waiting. Friends are there waiting and wanting to help you to climb a mountain again or scale a new summit.

Up ahead there's a bright light. There's hope, and love and new frontiers of exciting prospect. Move ahead and never give up; that's the trick; never give up.

You Will Dream Again

No matter where you live or what handicaps you face, you can succeed. No town is so small that it can keep you from winning. No past failure can keep you from winning. Youth can't stop you, nor can old age. It's never too early to start, nor is it ever too late to begin anew.

You don't have to be a *loser.* You *can* be a winner. And, you can start today. In thirty days you can make great strides. In sixty days everyone will notice drastic improvement. In six months you can have advanced so far that you will have a whole new and exciting life. You can win. Don't let anyone tell you that you can't be a winner. Don't let anyone tell you that it's too late for you.

Never give up

that's the trick

never give up

Other Books By Dr. Armstrong

These books are all available from Amazon.com. Go to Amazon, and on Amazon's search type in:

Kenneth Shelby Armstrong Books. Select the book that you want and pay Amazon.

To contact the author.

Author: Kenneth Shelby Armstrong Th.D., Ed.D.

Email: KennethWrites@me.com

.Web site..   www.ArmstrongBooks.com/

Phone: 1-580-873-2377

Write him. 1036 Holiday Acres Drive Fort Towson, OK 74735

KENNETH SHELBY ARMSTRONG

WHAT EVER
HAPPENED TO
ROBIN?

Whatever Happened to Robin?

On the shores of Lake Biwa near Kyoto, Japan, a distinguished American bishop laid his head in the lap of a lovely Japanese woman and died.

His death opened a secret that he had held since he was a young G.I. exploring the ruins of Hiroshima and Nagasaki with a young Japanese girl friend. The explosion of the secret shook a prominent American family and its church.

When he left Japan he promised to return and marry the girl of his dreams, but circumstances caused him to break that promise. Nevertheless, each New Year's Day he wrote her letters reaffirming his love and promising to return to her.

For decades he served his church as Bishop, but he never gave up his pledge to return to Robin. Nearing death he could delay no longer so he, used what strength he had to return to Japan and he laid his head in the lap of a lovely woman and died. But, to know the real secret you must read Whatever Happened to Robin?.

WILL IT BE DANGEROUS

Who is more prejudiced?
White people or Black people

KENNETH SHELBY ARMSTRONG

Will it Be Dangerous?

"No! No! No! You're looking at this thing all wrong. This will be a great educational experience. Just think of it! It's 1953 and segregation is the law of the State of Georgia and most other States in the South.

"A white graduate student walks into an all-negro University, say Atlanta University, and tries to enroll. What do you think would happen? This could be a life-changing experience for you, and it could bring about real change."

"That's what I'm thinking about. This life-changing experiment could get me killed. Have you ever heard of the Ku Klux Klan? If they hear about this I will be dead meat. If by some miracle the university should let me in, they will be breaking the law. It's illegal for them to accept a white student. I could even go to jail. I could get killed. And what if your Dean heard that you were advising one of your students to break the law?

"It could get you fired. But why should I worry? I'll be dead."

The story of the book is, that I did get enrolled and I'm still alive and significantly more educated.

HOW TO STRIVE, THRIVE, AND STAY ALIVE IN PRISON

KENNETH SHELBY ARMSTRONG Th.D., Ed.D.

How To Strive, Thrive, and Stay Alive in Prison

More than a million prisoners are now behind bars; eating three bland meals a day with never a change; each night they are serenaded by a chorus of snores from which there is no escape; they spend time in planning revenge on some member of their families or some policeman or judge who did them wrong; they wait for that special letter that never comes.

Too often mail call is a downer. It's a tough life for the men, but much harder on the women.

Broken dreams become nightmares. Soft memories are crushed by harsh treatment from detention officials. Visiting hours are too brief and saying goodbye to family and small children erupts in tears that will continue for hours.

But some in prison find forgiveness and others discover that there is hope. Some discover beauty in unexpected places. Faith, hope, and love, live there too.

My Very Best Stories

There is a really great editor/owner of the newspaper in the town where I live. He knows everybody and everybody knows him. In these days there are few towns and newspapers like the one we have in Hugo, Oklahoma.

I read his editorials every day and hidden inside of each one is pungent information, sparkling humor, and honest concern for the town where he has lived all of his life, and which many of us have adopted.

Against all odds he has kept our newspaper something that we look forward to getting. One day he asked me to let him publish some of my short stories in the paper. I gladly accepted the assignment. It was so well received that we decided to publish those stories in a book.

It's now available and the range of interest is broad enough to capture the interest of people even though they live in New York City or Los Angeles. These are stories for everyone.

KENNETH SHELBY
ARMSTRONG

I WAS A
RELUCTANT
GUEST

I Was a Reluctant Guest

Being in prison can be an exciting adventure. Every inmate has some great story to tell–and that over and over again. But the stories that come from prison are rooted in a minutia of facts, most of which are boring and void of meaning.

The facts of each prisoner's case may be interesting only to a weird attorney or some other prisoner who is looking for some way to get out. What do you do when you are looking at twenty years in each dreadful place?

Of more interest than facts are the emotions and feelings alive in each prison. For the most part the emotions are kept within specifically prescribed boundaries, but too often they spill out like volcanic ash. The results can be fights, riots, and escapes.

Neither guards nor reluctant guests look forward to such events. But you will begin to understand the drama of prison, inside and out.

He Died a Hero

In our current culture a hero is someone, dressed in a cape and flying through the air with the greatest of ease to release some damsel who has gotten into the clutches of an ogre with warts. Of course the drama takes place on some remote planet located just above Kansas City.

The plot is compelling and people will pay $15 just to experience the unreality of some weirdo's imagination. On the other hand an unadorned reality is a country boy wearing patched overalls and sporting a straw hat with holes in the brim and a black sweat band earned while picking cotton under an Oklahoma sun, to earn a few cents to put bread on the table during the peak of the Great Depression.

After supper he will study until his eye lids shut his brain down, but he is committed to getting a college education–the first in his family.

With the diploma placed in the back pocket of his overalls he marched out to serve his God and those in need. What a Story!

The Win With Wisdom Series

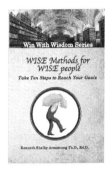

These books are available at AMAZON BOOKS.
They are also available directly from the author for $6.00 each.
==
Special Offer:
The entire collection of 6 books are offered for $25.00
if purchased directly from the author. In addition the author will
pay shipping and handling costs. This special offer is extended
only for a short time. To order write:

Dr. Kenneth Shelby Armstrong
1036 Holiday Acres Dr.
Fort Towson, OK 74735   Or Call: 1-580-873-2377

80858537R00066

Made in the USA
San Bernardino, CA
02 July 2018